S0-CWY-142

JoAn Stevenson
Illustrations by Kim Hanzo

TEACUP PRESS

Copyright © 2021 by JoAn Stevenson

All rights reserved. Published in the United States by Teacup Press, an imprint of Fox Pointe Publishing, LLP. No part of this book may be reproduced in any form or by any electronic or mechanical means, including information storage and retrieval systems, without permission in writing from the publisher.

www.teacup-press.com • www.foxpointepublishing.com/author-jo-an-stevenson

Library of Congress Cataloging-in-Publication Data
Stevenson, JoAn, author.
Farr, Chelsea, editor.
Hanzo, Kim, illustrator.
Hudson, Becca, designer.

You / JoAn Stevenson. – First edition.

Summary: An illustrated poem about a parent or guardian's love for their child.

ISBN 978-1-952567-32-2 (hardcover) / 978-1-952567-31-5 (softcover)
[1. Multigenerational Family Life – Fiction. 2. Emotions & Feelings – Fiction. 3. Poetry – Fiction.]

Library of Congress Control Number: 2 0 2 1 9 0 5 7 7 3
Printed and bound in the United States of America by Lakeside Press Inc.

First printing May 2021

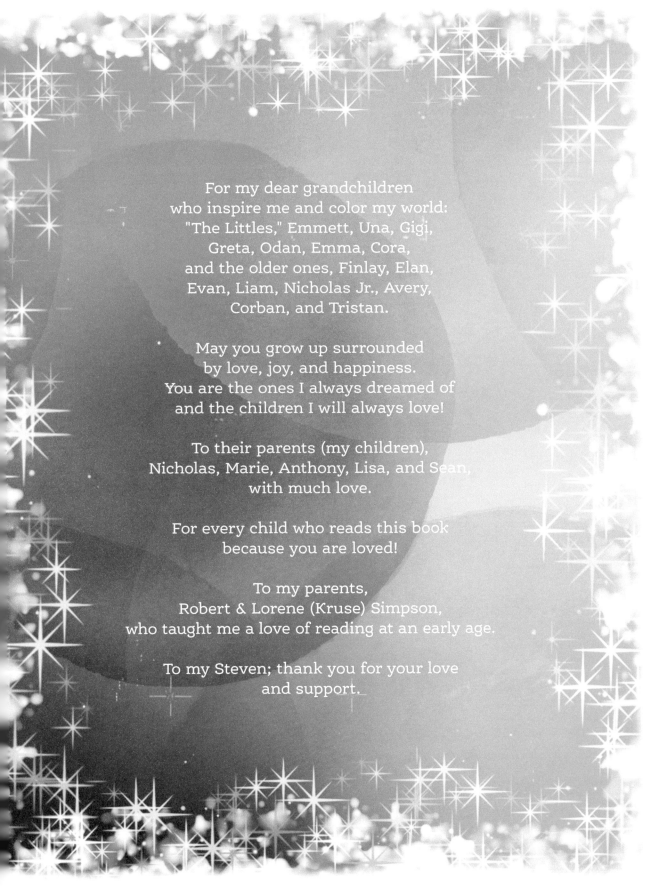

For my dear grandchildren
who inspire me and color my world:
"The Littles," Emmett, Una, Gigi,
Greta, Odan, Emma, Cora,
and the older ones, Finlay, Elan,
Evan, Liam, Nicholas Jr., Avery,
Corban, and Tristan.

May you grow up surrounded
by love, joy, and happiness.
You are the ones I always dreamed of
and the children I will always love!

To their parents (my children),
Nicholas, Marie, Anthony, Lisa, and Sean,
with much love.

For every child who reads this book
because you are loved!

To my parents,
Robert & Lorene (Kruse) Simpson,
who taught me a love of reading at an early age.

To my Steven; thank you for your love
and support.

You are the *favorite* story I always tell.

You are the **wish** in the wishing well.

You are the kite
are the
flying high
in the sky.

You are the
huckleberry
in the pie.

3

You

are the

yellow

dandelion
chain.

4

You are the
rainbow
after the rain.

You
are the
lucky
penny
I found

and
the *book*
that
I
can't
put
down.

You are the *firefly* dancing in the breeze

and
the
songbird
singing from
the trees.

10

You
are the
peanut
butter
and the **jelly**

and the
deep
laugh
that comes
from my belly.

You are the *grass* tickling my feet

and my *favorite song* with the groovy beat.

12

You

are the

candles

on the
birthday
cake.

You are the

morning mist

on the lake.

You
are the
paint
colorfully
swirled.

You are the

seven
wonders

of my world.

You
are the
lightning
and the
thunder
and the
umbrella
I take shelter under.

You
are the
owl
hooting in the night.

You are the
moonbeam
glowing so bright.

You are the one I always dreamed of and the child that I will always love.

about the author

JoAn Stevenson is a fifth-generation Iowan and is now beginning a retirement career of writing books, mainly in the genres of children's and poetry. She has always been an avid reader and believes this is why she took up writing decades ago. Every year, she and her family members submit poems to the annual publication, "Lyrical Iowa."

JoAn has five children and several grandchildren. She lives with three cats and enjoys reading, knitting, traveling, cooking, gardening, biking, and volunteering. Her favorite color is blue and she adores apple pie, Italian food, and potatoes in any form!

about the illustrator

Kim Hanzo is a graphic designer and illustrator who specializes in animal-inspired stories and imagery. She graduated from the Rochester Institute of Technology with a BFA in Illustration and an MFA in Painting. She has been a graphic designer for more than twenty years and founded her own greeting cards and prints company, Lellow Lolly, in 2016. Her work is available online and in several Hallmark stores in the US Southeast. Kim joined Fox Pointe Publishing in 2020 as a children's book illustrator. She also writes and illustrates her own children's books, including the "World of Difference" series starring animals with meaningful messages. She lives in North Carolina with her husband, three kids, mother, two dogs, four fish, and one guinea pig.

ALSO BY AUTHOR
JoAn Stevenson

LATE SIDE OF MIDNIGHT

$18.95 ($24.89 CAN)
978-1-952567-33-9
Hardcover

foxpointepublishing.com/
shop-now/late-side-of-
midnight-hardcover

$12.95 ($17.01 CAN)
978-1-952567-46-9
Softcover

foxpointepublishing.com/
shop-now/late-side-of-
midnight-softcover

Teacup Press
Fox Pointe Publishing, LLP